New Habits New Wealth

How Changing Some Habits Can Improve Your Personal Health And Financial Wealth

Other Books by R and R

Meditation for beginners
What is Meditation and how can it change your life? A Guide to mindfulness and happiness.

F*ck Motivation
It's your life. A guide on how to live your life and be happy.

Declutter
A beginners 10 step guide on how to simplify your file by decluttering.

New Habits - New Wealth
How changing some habits can improve your personal health and financial wealth.

Puppy Training
Top 10 ideas for training your dog within a month to keep everybody in your house happy and stress free.

Minimalist
The How To and Why of becoming a minimalist

www.randrdigitallifestyle.com

Introduction

We all have some habits that we are not proud of that we want to break as well as other good habits that we want to nurture. Unfortunately, most people think breaking habits is like flipping a switch, i.e., that you just decide to quit smoking and you do or decide to start waking up early, and you simply do it.

Here is the thing; habits don't just disappear. You're not going to wake up one day and find that you now hate cigarettes. Yes, you may let go of the habit for a while maybe because your mind is preoccupied with other things at the moment but unless you've made conscious efforts to break or alter a habit, it never really goes away.

So, yes, you're stuck with that damaging habit for the rest of your life until you do something about it. Unfortunately, 'doing something about it' is not always as easy as it sounds. When something becomes a habit, it's more or less like an addiction.

Moreover, learning a new habit is not easier either because the human brain doesn't really like 'hard work.' You need to be deliberate and to sort of 'hack' your brain if you really want your mind to 'get used' to engaging in a specific habit. If you've tried breaking bad habits and building new ones unsuccessfully, you know that it is not a walk in the park. We know you also understand just how frustrating it can get.

However, the process doesn't have to be complicated; you can learn the whole process and successfully build any new habit while breaking any bad habit. And this book will give you the necessary framework to follow to help you break any bad habit and build any good habit.

In simple terms, the book will demystify the habit learning process.

You'll discover:

- How to break bad habits

- How to learn new habits easily

- The habits of successful, healthy and happy people that you can also learn

- And much more

Let's begin!

Thanks again for purchasing this book. We hope you enjoy it! – R & R

Table of Contents

Chapter 1

Why Habits Matter

It's not that you don't know what the problem is or what's been holding you back. Of course, you know that smoking will damage your lungs. You know that procrastination is bad for you. You're aware that impulsive spending will leave you poor, and binge-eating will destroy your health.

You know these things; you know some of your habits are bad and will potentially destroy you; you've always known.

But what you don't know is how to break away from these habits.

You've made several New Year, New Month and even New Week resolutions but failed.

You've set goals, but nothing has come out of it.

You've tried desperately to improve yourself and make changes more times than you can count, but still, everything stays the same.

The truth is, you are not in control of your life- your habits are.

Steven Kaas once said:

> *"You are not the king of your brain. You are the creepy guy standing next to the king going "a most judicious choice, Sire"*

Chris Sparks of The Medium puts it better:

> *"With habits, free will is an illusion. Half of our daily actions are actually predetermined by context, and performed unconsciously. Our perception of conscious control is a backwards-facing rationalization designed to protect our ego and retrofit a messy reality into a cleaner narrative".*

You are not in control of most of the actions you take daily; your brain controls you through your habits, and you can't see any transformations in your life, mindset or behaviors if you don't work on your habits and here's why:

Habits Are The Foundation Of Success

Habits put your life on autopilot. They determine how your body works and responds to things every single day.

Habits make you become like a machine or a computer that has been programmed to function in a certain way. If you try to make that machine work in a different way that it's not used to, it will start giving you error messages. Some machines would even shut down to protect themselves from compromise or damage. That's what habits do to you.

You may know that the right thing to do is to brush your teeth before you sleep, but if you've built a habit of sleeping without cleaning your teeth every night, it will take a lot of willpower for you to really get yourself to do that no matter how good it is for you.

At the same time, if you've formed a habit of cleaning your teeth before bed every night, it's going to be really hard if you don't clean your teeth before you sleep.

In fact, you won't give too much thought to it; you just find yourself doing it because your body has been programmed to do just that.

So if you want to make your life better, if you want to be successful, healthy and happy, you have to program yourself through your habits to act in ways that will help you become what you want to be, and your body will just keep running on autopilot, doing the right things. Even when you are tempted to act in a way that will jeopardize your goals, your brain will send out that 'error message' and automatically help you stick to doing what is right for you.

One Positive Habit Can Lead to Several Positive Changes in Your Life

Habits mostly have a domino effect.

Sometimes all it takes is to break one bad habit or develop one good habit, and you'll find yourself making several other positive changes in your life. Waking up early every morning, for instance, is a positive habit. If you've had the bad habit of staying in bed for too long, it takes a lot of productive time away from you; time to exercise, meditate, write your daily to-do list, cook and eat a healthy breakfast, so you don't have to rely on unhealthy takeout and go to work early, so you're feeling relaxed and energetic by the time you get to work.

Staying in bed too late will probably just have you waking up 20 -30 minutes to work time, and you'll have to rush through breakfast and dress up and spend the rest of the time trying to beat traffic so you can get to work early.

When you eventually get to work, you're already spent from the stress, and that takes something off your productivity levels for the day. If you're able to break that bad habit of waking up late, it allows you to develop other good, helpful morning habits that can make you successful and more fulfilled.

If you develop a morning exercise habit, it can motivate you to cultivate other healthy morning habits like drinking a smoothie, meditating every morning, and so on. One good habit can trigger the onset of dozens of other good habits that will change your life for good. The thing is; successful people didn't just become successful; they had to do something about their habits.

All Successful People Had to Do Something about Their Habits

Steven Pressfield once said, *"The difference between an amateur and a professional is in the habits. An amateur has amateur habits. A professional has professional habits"*.

The difference between successful people and failures is in their habits. Every successful person you've heard of had to develop some unique habits that they credit for their success.

Famous writer, Mary Higgins Clark, had to develop a habit of waking up at 4am and 5am every morning to write because she discovered that there were too many distractions at other hours of the day, and those hours were the best times she had to pursue a successful writing career.

Demison Hatch wrote bestselling books while holding a 9-5 job. He had to form a habit of writing 500 words a day before starting his day job. This was how he wrote his first three best-selling novels.

Benjamin Franklin had to form a habit of working long hours every day. He typically worked from 5am to 10pm every day. He credited this habit for helping him grow his printing business.

Greek Orator, Demosthenes, had a habit of shaving off half of his hair, so he was never tempted to leave his home without composing his orations. This was how he conquered the habit of procrastination.

Arianna Huffington, after collapsing from exhaustion some years ago, had to take out all the electronics in her room so she could get eight hours of sleep every night.

President Obama had a habit of staying up till after 2am every day to get most of his work done.

Name any famous, successful person, and they'll tell you how they had to cut out some habits or form new ones, and how it's mostly responsible for their success or contributed significantly. This essentially means good habits can help you reach your goals, as we will find out next.

Good Habits Help You Reach Your Goals

If you want to win your city's marathon, you're not just going to wake up one morning, jump on the tracks and win the marathon. It's going to take months; if not years of training, to develop the skills and agility that will help you win a marathon. It will also take establishing a regular training habit to be able to develop those skills.

If you want to shed 80 pounds, you're not just going to wake up one morning to see the fat melt away. You'll have to form the right set of habits- healthy eating, regular workouts, etc., and commit to it over a long period of time before you even start to see any real changes.

Every motivational speaker, life coach, or talk show host tells you how you have to set goals if you want to attain success, but goals are useless without the habits to back them up. Goals are just mere wishful thinking; habits are what will get the work done. How does it all add up?

Let us explain:

1: Habits Increase Efficiency

As humans, we are programmed in a way that our brains try to avoid hard work or anything difficult or challenging. We find ourselves thinking and pondering on it for hours or days when we have to handle difficult tasks.

Some of us just procrastinate until it's no longer possible for us to run away from the task. Building habits; however, will make you more efficient by automating your tasks so that you don't have to overthink about it or be tempted to procrastinate.

2: Habits Can Replace Motivation

On days when you just don't feel like it- when you don't feel like working, exercising, or eating healthy, good habits can come through for you because when something becomes a habit for you, you don't need a lot of motivation to act.

What exactly is this thing called habit? Let's discuss that next.

Chapter 2

What are Habits?

Habits are those things you do daily or rituals you perform automatically without thinking much about them. Do you wake up in the morning to drink a cup of water? That's a habit. Do you pray or meditate every morning? That's a habit.

Do you stay in bed until it is 30 minutes to work before jumping up and trying to get prepared for work in a hurry? That's a habit too. Or maybe you always get drunk before 9 am in the morning? That's also a habit.

Everything you do regularly is a habit. You can also think of habits as something that you cannot do without.

Do you find it difficult to sleep at night without taking a shower? That's because taking a shower has become a habit for you, so when you skip it, it's always going to feel like something is amiss. Sometimes you'll even find yourself getting up in the middle of the night to take that shower because you've not been able to sleep comfortably and after the shower, you just sleep like a baby.

So, whatever you do or cannot do without regularly is a habit.

You can also think of habits as anything that you do automatically without having to overthink about it before doing it. If you clean your teeth or shower every morning, you don't need to set an alarm to remind yourself that you have to clean your teeth or take a shower- everything just comes naturally to you because you've probably been doing this since you were a little child, so it's already become a habit.

What about driving?

When you start learning how to drive, you're very careful. Your mind is always 100% on the wheels and all the controls in the car because you don't want to make a mistake. You'll also have to continue to remind yourself *"Okay, there's a bump ahead, I have to slow down and use the brakes"*, *"I'm going to make a left turn up there, I have to slow down"*, *"I'm approaching a junction, I have to signal to alert other drivers"*. You have to keep reminding yourself of what to do because the entire process is still very new to you.

We can remember our own experience and how friends used to laugh because if they passed by on the road, we were always too scared to look sideways to say hello to them. We were always looking ahead like something was going to go terribly wrong if we took our eyes off the road for as much as a second. The car had to be very quiet; no music, and you better not try to talk to because it was very distracting. Today, we can literally drive some routes with our eyes shut, especially from work to home and back. This is a route we drive through every day, and it has become a habit for us. Everything happens with very little or no conscious thoughts - we can listen to loud music, we can take calls using the hands free device, we can say hello to people and even look at billboards and roadside attractions without causing an accident because driving has become a habit and the entire process is now registered in our subconscious mind.

How Are Habits Formed?

Two things form a person's habits:

- Your Thoughts
- Your Actions

There's an old quote by Lao Tzu that goes:

Watch your thoughts, they become your words

Watch your words, they become actions

Watch your actions, they become habits

Watch your habits, they become character

Watch your character, it becomes your destiny

From this quote, we see that everything starts from the mind; from your thoughts.

Your thoughts drive you, they determine the actions that you take and your actions, when consistently done over a period of time, becomes your habits.

The American Journal of Psychology defines habits as *"a more or less fixed way of thinking, willing or feeling acquired through previous repetition of a mental experience."*

Your thoughts build your habits.

If you're a regular coffee drinker or a coffee addict, we can bet that you weren't born with a coffee drinking habit. It started one day, and it began with a conscious thought that you gave life to via your actions.

Maybe you were standing at a train station waiting for your train one day, and you saw a coffee stand, and you thought *"Oh, that coffee smells nice, I should buy one."* And then you got a cup and drunk it on the train. The next day you were at the train station, and you saw the coffee stand again and your thoughts acted again *"Yesterday's coffee was nice, I'll just get one today."* And then you did the same thing on the third, fourth, fifth, sixth, and seventh day and other days after that. What you were doing, in that case, was building a habit. It happened at a psychological level;

you were responding to your thoughts, but as you did that, you were creating something called a trigger.

Every time you saw a coffee stand, got a coffee and then drank it, you were subconsciously creating a trigger in your brain such that every time you saw a coffee stand or you were at the train station, or even onboard a train, your subconscious mind reminded you that you need to buy a coffee.

Why?

Because your brain had already become accustomed to the pleasure (reward), you derive from drinking coffee. Your subconscious mind associated the taste of coffee with pleasure because you enjoyed drinking coffee every day.

So even when you forgot, or were not in the mood for coffee, or on days when you were too broke to buy yourself a cup, the triggers created by your brain's pleasure-reward centers had already been activated. They'll always remind you and make you feel like something is not yet complete when you did not have your coffee.

Gradually, you started finding yourself getting a morning coffee without thinking about it- you just found yourself walking to the stand to get coffee every time you were at the train station. And even on days when you were not at the train station, your subconscious mind still reminded you that you've not had coffee that day, so you looked for someplace else to get that cup of coffee.

At this stage, the habit formation process was complete, and it takes another series of conscious thoughts and consistent actions to break that habit.

The above is a simplified version of how habits form. There is a scientific explanation to that, which we will discuss next.

Scientific Explanations For How Habits Are Formed

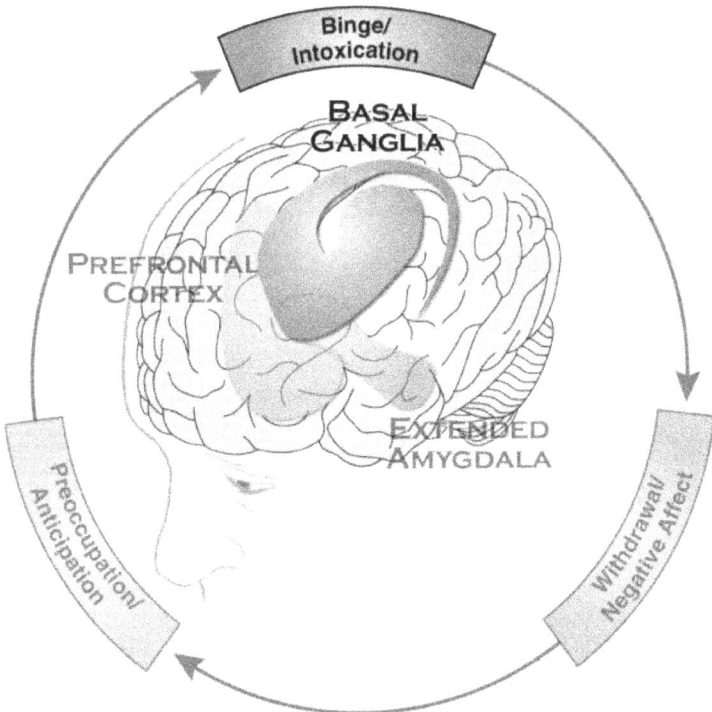

Why do consistent actions become subconscious habits?

It's because the human brain is literally jam-packed. Your brain coordinates a bulk of tasks that keep you alive and functioning as a normal human being every day. Digestion, respiration, excretion, emotions, memories, pattern recognition, communication; all of these complex processes and many more are coordinated by your brain every single second of the day- that's a lot of work.

Neuroscientists explain that because of the multiple tasks that the brain has to perform daily, it's always looking for functions that it can automate so that its workload will be reduced, so to speak.

A part of the brain called the basal ganglia tries to automate some of the things you do regularly. The prefrontal cortex is responsible for decision making. Before an activity becomes a habit, the prefrontal cortex has to be involved in helping you make conscious decisions to do that stuff, but once the basal ganglia registers it as a habit, the prefrontal cortex literally takes a hands-off approach. That's why you no longer get to think about the task or make any conscious decisions before you perform the habit.

Charles Duhigg, the author of The Power of Habit and a Business Writer at the New York Times explains *"You can do these complex behaviors without being mentally aware of it at all, and that's because of the capacity of our Basal Ganglia to take a behavior and turn it into an automatic routine.......in fact, the brain starts working less and less.*

The brain can almost completely shut down and this is a real advantage because it means you have all of this mental activity you can devote to something else. That's why it's easy- while driving, or parallel parking, let's say to entirely focus on something else; like the radio, or a conversation you're having".

However, the basal ganglia cannot create habits on its own without the help of a third part of the brain called the Amygdala.

Before something can become a habit- that's before the basal ganglia can automate a task or activity, it has to be something that gives you some kind of pleasurable experience.

Banging your head against the wall, for instance, cannot become a habit because it creates an unpleasant experience for you. Your brain will not automate such actions; instead, it will trigger a fight or flight response so that you can avoid that activity.

But taking alcohol or opiates is a different experience; you get high, and your emotional state is altered- you're happy, and your brain can feel that this particular activity gives a pleasurable experience-that's the one our brain automates and makes into a habit.

Now you're probably saying *"What about people who have a habit of hurting themselves? Like people who are addicted to body piercing, tattoos, or even banging their heads against the wall?"*

Well, here's an exercise for you- try to pinch yourself slightly on the arm for a minute, what did you notice? First, you felt a sharp pain, but as the pinch got longer, you no longer felt the pain.

That's something that happens to people who have formed a habit of hurting themselves. There's a reason why they started doing it- may be to vent their frustrations or whatever it is so they are able to endure the pain in exchange for the reward (the reason why they are doing it) and eventually, they become immune to the pain as their brain helps to numb it and focus on the reward.

This is why bad habits, even though you know they will potentially destroy you, are tough to break. A junk-eating habit can kill you but your brain doesn't care about that; it only cares about the pleasure you get when you eat junk and doesn't want you to feel miserable or suffer serious cravings like you always do when you don't get your fill of your favorite burger or that favorite dessert.

Procrastinating is a habit that can make you poor and completing tasks has a lot of ultimate rewards but your brain doesn't like the stress you have to go through to get the work done, so it doesn't automate task completion but automates checking your social media updates so that when you want to do difficult, *unpleasant tasks* like actually getting some work done, it triggers the habit of surfing the internet instead.

So you see, you are not in charge of your habits- yes, you can stop blaming yourself now.

Yes, you created those habits, but as soon as the Basal Ganglia took over, the controls left your hands and try as you might to stop that habit, you can't do anything on your own until you apply some mental techniques to force your brain to give up that habit.

In the next chapter, you'll find out what these mental techniques are and how to use them to break your bad habits.

Chapter 3

The Easiest Way to Change Old Habits

They say old habits die hard, and that may be true, but it may only be hard but not impossible to alter old habits.

Every habit has three elements:

- A cue

- A routine

- A reward

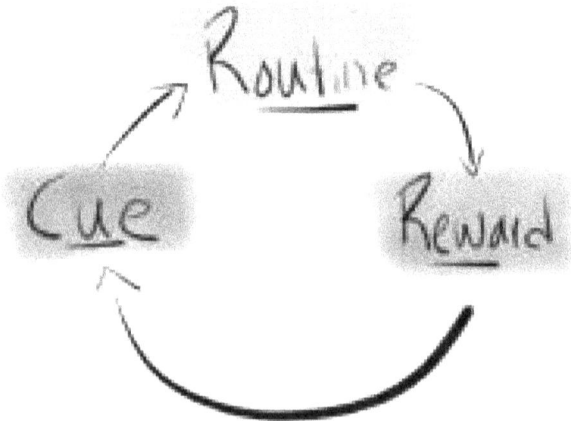

And the key to breaking any bad habits lie with these three key elements.

The Cue

A cue is anything that triggers a habit- anything that causes you to take a particular action. If you always eat or crave for a bag of chips every time you're watching a movie at home, then watching a movie is your cue for the habit of eating chips.

If you always smoke or feel the need to smoke every time you're lonely, then being lonely is your cue for smoking. From our example in the previous chapter, being on the train is a cue for the habit of drinking coffee.

A cue is anything that prompts you or reminds you to take a particular course of action, and it can be anything; your cue can be a location, the people you are around, your emotional state, a time of day- anything at all.

Before any habit is formed, there has to be a cue- something that prompted you to take that action in the first place, and once your Basal Ganglia registers a habit, it also records the cue.

The cue is what your brain uses to inform the rest of your body that it's time to take a particular action. And the more you respond to the cue, the more the connection between the cue and the habit become stronger and difficult to break.

If you're a masturbator for instance, and you always do it when no one is home, on days when you didn't plan to masturbate or never even thought of masturbating, as soon as you're alone at home, your brain starts reminding you *"Hey, you know no one's home now, it's time to do that thing you always do- that thing you always enjoy"*.

Cues are very potent.

Routines

Routines are the actual actions you take in response to the cue. Masturbating, for instance, is a routine. Smoking is a routine.

Any habit or action that you find yourself doing regularly is a routine.

Reward

There is no habit without a reward. If your brain or body is not getting some type of pleasure from an action, it's not going to become a habit. We already discussed this in the previous chapter. Masturbation, for instance, causes the release of internal chemicals like dopamine, serotonin, and endorphins.

These chemicals give temporary relief and escape from stress, difficult emotions, insomnia, and other struggles. Masturbation has the same effect that some recreational drugs have on the body, and this is a reward for the brain.

Binge-eating and procrastination also have their rewards. Procrastination helps you avoid the heavy lifting for a while. When you procrastinate, you opt for fun things, or you laze around instead of doing hard work and this your brain considers a reward because you're actually doing things you enjoy rather than the ones that scare you or put your brain and body under stress.

Binge-eating and food addiction also have rewards for the brain. Binge-eating also triggers the release of Dopamine in the brain, and dopamine provides temporary pleasure.

So, every good or bad habit has its rewards, and the reward is why the brain automates the action and makes it into a habit.

Note that rewards are not always tangible or physical. Most times, you don't even know what's going on up there. You just realize one day that something you did once or twice has suddenly become a habit that you're finding hard to break away from.

It's just like how you don't see the oxygen that you inhale, but it's happening in the background- you're breathing.

So how do you break bad habits with all we've discussed in mind? Let's discuss that.

How to Break Bad Habits

To break bad habits, you have to do the following:

- **Isolate the Cue**: You have to identify the trigger and understand what is causing you to act that way.

  Note that it's not going to happen overnight; you'll have to spend a few weeks studying yourself and recording your habits before you can correctly isolate the cue to your bad habits.

  So, get yourself a journal and record these details for the next 21 days.

  Do not try to fight or change the habit at this stage, just record.

Name of Bad Habit:	
Location (Where are you when you do it?)	
Time	
Emotional state (How/what were you feeling like before you did it?)	
People (Who else was around you when you did it?)	
What actions immediately preceded the urge?	
How did you feel immediately after you did it?	
What did you do immediately after you did it?	

This will help you identify patterns and help you identify your cues. Perhaps being around some people triggers a bad habit or you always feel the urge at a specific time of day, or maybe it always happened when you are feeling a certain way.

- **Identify The Routine**: The journal will also help you understand the routine better. What exactly do you do? How do you do it? What do you do before and after you do that habit?

- **Identify The Rewards:** Identifying the rewards is also essential. Some masturbators, for instance, say it helps them sleep (that's a valid reward). Some people can't function at their day jobs without caffeine- better productivity at work is the reward for caffeine here.

You have to identify what you're really getting out of that habit and to do that, you have to track:

  - Your Actions after The Act

  - Your Feelings after The Act

Identifying the reward will help you break the habit because if masturbation is what enables you to sleep, you can start figuring out healthier habits that can help you sleep, so you don't have to use bad, damaging or unsavory actions to achieve your goals.

Now armed with all the necessary information, this is how you break bad habits.

- **Choose a Substitute Habit**: It's almost impossible to break a bad habit without replacing it with another habit because your brain will literally bug you to death to indulge in that bad habit because not doing the action creates a void. It's out of character, and the best way to tackle it is to fill up that void by substituting your bad habit with a good one.

So to substitute:

- o Identify the reward (the end goal)

- o Find out healthier ways to achieve the end goal

- o Substitute the bad habit for a good one

So if you want to break the habit of binge-eating, for instance, you identify the reward, e.g., it helps you cope with emotional stress.

What are some of the healthier ways to cope with emotional stress?

- o Breathing exercises

- o Taking a long walk

So you substitute the habit of binge eating with taking a hike or doing breathing exercises.

- **Eliminate The Cues**: Like we said earlier, there's always something that triggers your bad habits, and when you've identified what that thing is, you either eliminate the cue or you manage it.

  If being alone makes you masturbate, then avoid being alone or open the doors and windows when you are alone at home, so there's no chance to do anything sneaky.

If checking social media first thing in the morning causes you to procrastinate, then don't check social media in the morning.

If the cues are things that you cannot eliminate, then manage it. To manage your triggers, you have to expect it and then call it.

The Journal you made would already give you enough information about your habits so when you're in that location that triggers your bad habits, or it is that time of the day when you always do it, you can anticipate and use your will power to fight the habit.

However, it's always easier to manipulate the cue and use it as a trigger for the good, alternative habits you want to form because it takes a lot of willpower to stop yourself from indulging in an activity that your brain enjoys.

Announce Your Goals and Choose an Accountability Partner

Nobody wants to be seen as a failure- everyone wants people around them to respect and admire them and see them as achievers. You can use this to your advantage when trying to break bad habits. Look for people who respect you, look up to you and praise you, and boast to them. Yes, tell everyone how you're going to stop your bad habits. It's only natural that you won't want them to lose the respect that they have for you so you'll want to keep up with working to break the habits you already told the world that you were going to do away with.

However, there are some poor habits that you can't admit to most people that you have. For these types of habits, an accountability partner that you trust- like your spouse, your best friend(s) or your kids can serve as an accountability partner and they can help you stay focused on kicking your bad habits.

Surround Yourself with People of Like Minds

You are as good as the people you hang out with. The kind of people you surround yourself with, to a large extent, determine how successful you're going to become in life. We have been lucky to have met successful people who inspired us to make drastic changes.

The friends we hang around with when we are young are often the '*everything's gonna be alright*' kind of people. They were very hard working and kind people, but we didn't get any motivation or inspiration from them. If anything, they made us feel like we were doing okay because there was always this feeling of *"But Mark's not doing any better, so it's not us, it's the economy."*

It's time to start surrounding yourself with the people who have the exact habits that you want to develop- this is the fastest way for anyone to form new habits because the influence that friends have on you is very powerful- *that's why your momma always warned you about peer pressure.*

Now use the peer pressure to your own advantage.

Visualize your Success

There's a lifestyle you are aiming for- there are results you want to achieve. Your bad habits are standing in the way of those results but if only you can continuously remind yourself of the destination, the goal and how much pleasure you're going to get from achieving your goals, it won't be so hard to commit to breaking the bad habits.

What you should do is to print a photo of your goals, or get something that can continuously remind you of what you're trying to achieve. Take that reminder and stick it in your workspace, use it as your phone and computer screen saver; stick it everywhere, so you're constantly reminded of the reason why you've decided to break the bad habits, and you're always motivated to keep up with the good habits.

Use Positive Affirmations

Come up with strong positive phrases that you can use to counter strong urges for bad habits. The phrase should be something that can remind you of the goal and the consequences at the same time.

Example: *'If I don't get up to exercise today, I'll continue to be obese, and I'm not going to be able to improve my self-confidence."*

Now come up with your own set of positive affirmations that'll help you commit to breaking those negative habits you want to break.

Don't Beat Yourself up When You Slip Up

It's inevitable, you're going to slip up sometimes and go back to doing that thing you thought you would never do again. Sometimes it'll happen almost as soon as you start working to break the habit and at other times it will happen at a time when you thought you had successfully kicked the bad habit- like maybe a year after or several months after.

This kind of scenario can be very disappointing, but it's not uncommon- it happens a lot to even the best of us.

So when it happens, know that it's part of the process and forgive yourself immediately. Don't use that as an excuse to fall back into your old ways- just forget about what has happened and continue to work on breaking those bad habits like you've been doing before.

Plan for Failures

Lastly, you should have a strategic plan for managing failures. The truth is, it might take more than one attempt to successfully kick a bad habit. So the question is, what are you going to do on days when you slip up? What is your 'disaster' management plan? It helps to plan ahead for the low times, especially by devising a motivational strategy for yourself to help you get right back on track when you slip up.

Now that you know how to break bad habits let's focus on how to build good habits.

Chapter 4

How to Choose and Form New Habits

Don't just choose habits because they are good - Mark wakes up at 5am everyday, so I have to start doing the same. Meanwhile, you work evening shifts and don't leave work until 11 pm whereas; Mark leaves work at 4pm and sleeps comfortably through the night. You're going to end up exhausted while Mark will be healthy and happy because he's getting enough rest while you're not.

Habits should be customized- they should be about you and what's going to help you achieve your goals- what's going to help you live a fulfilled life and go to your grave a happy person.

Why are you trying to form new habits? Because you want to do better than you already are- you want to be successful.

So the new habits you form should be habits that can help you achieve what you really want to achieve. If you're trying to become a Millionaire by the time you're 50 for instance, the habits you need to develop would be different from that of a person whose goal is to publish three bestselling books before they are 30. A person who wants to become a millionaire by 50 will need to develop good savings and financial management habits. A person who is looking to write best sellers will probably just need to form a habit of writing a specific number of words daily, daily reading habits to expand their knowledge, and habits to help them avoid procrastination and deal with writer's block.

Your habits should always be tailored to your goals.

With that in mind, here's how to form habits that are tailored to your goals:

1. What are your dreams and goals?

Where are you headed? What are you trying to achieve? Who are you trying to become? Write all of your goals down.

2. What are those habits that will help you achieve all these goals?

If your goal is to lose weight, of course, you know that you have to develop healthy eating habits, regular workout habits, weight monitoring habits, and so on.

So what habits do you need to form to achieve your goals quickly?

You can use the table below to write down the habits you need for all your goals.

Goal 1	Habit 1 .... Habit 2 .... Habit 3...................... Habit 4...................... Habit 5 ....
Goal 2	Habit 1 .... Habit 2 .... Habit 3...................... Habit 4...................... Habit 5 ....
Goal 3	Habit 1 .... Habit 2 .... Habit 3...................... Habit 4...................... Habit 5 ....
Goal 4	Habit 1 .... Habit 2 .... Habit 3...................... Habit 4...................... Habit 5 ....

3. Automate your Habits

Remember we talked about how habits become automatic after some time?

This happens most of the time unconsciously, but it doesn't mean that you cannot consciously automate your habits. All it takes is to commit to a course of action for a period of time and your brain will automate it.

But since you're trying to form a couple of good habits the same time, the easiest way to do it is to create a ritual where one habit will serve as a trigger for another.

Let us explain;

In the previous chapter, we talked about habits loop and how habits become automated. We said some locations, sights, sounds, or actions can be a cue for a habit.

If an action can trigger another action, that means one action can lead you to perform another. It's just like driving a car- you don't have to remind yourself what to do "*I just turned on the ignition, now I have to step on the brakes, now I have to step on the gas and turn right, etc.*" It just comes automatically because you've been driving for a long time and you've been using a series of commands to get yourself to your destination, so it's become automatic- your brain already knows what comes next at every point in time.

If you always drink a glass of warm water when you wake up in the morning, waking up becomes a cue for drinking a glass of water. Every time you wake up, your brain will remind you that you have to drink water.

If the next thing you do after drinking a glass of warm water is to look at your face in the mirror, then every time you drink a glass of water, you'll find yourself going towards the mirror to look at your face.

If the next thing you do after that is to brush your teeth, you don't need to set a reminder because you find yourself brushing your teeth.

Similarly, if you're trying to form good habits, you can use one good habit as a cue for another.

If your goal is to lose weight, for instance, we'll assume that some of the habits you'll want to form will include:

Activity 1: Wake up early every morning by 5 a.m.

Activity 2: Drink a glass of warm water with half of a lemon.

Activity 3: Run for 30 minutes

Activity 4: Do cardio for 30 minutes

Activity 5: Drink a healthy smoothie

Activity 6: Eat a healthy breakfast

Activity 7: Pack a healthy lunch

So, for the next 3 months (90 days), you have to do all the activities that you've listed in the same order. Do activity 1 first thing in the morning and follow up immediately with activities 2, 3, 4, etc. as though you're a robot.

This creates a habit loop and helps your brain to automate all the tasks.

Give it about 90 days of consistency (according to Lally's study, it takes between 18 and 254 days for the human brain to pick up a consistent action and register it as a habit-this depends on the nature of the habit and the individual). So by the 90th day, your brain will probably have registered your new set of rituals as a habit loop, and you'll find yourself doing one action after the other without giving too much thought to it.

4. Create Rewards

Remember, there's no habit automation without reward. If there is no reward for your brain to look forward to, automating your new set of habits becomes difficult, if not impossible.

So, you have to use something that you really like and enjoy as a reward- something healthy. It doesn't have to be expensive; you could give yourself a little more extra time on social media, read your favorite books, stay in bed a little longer, spend time with friends, or see a movie on weekends when you didn't miss your habit loop during the week.

When you automate your habits, it becomes an addiction. So if you build good habits, you can consider them 'good addictions.' Well, addiction is farfetched, but we believe you get the point we're trying to pass along. We know you might be wondering; so which habits should you strive to build? Well, while you may have your own priorities of the habits you may want to build, you don't have to reinvent the wheel; you could just build the habits that successful, happy, wealthy and healthy people have, and you will essentially become like them. Let's discuss that next.

Chapter 5

The Habits of Successful, Wealthy, Healthy and Happy People

You already know how to develop good habits; the question now is "*Which good habits should you develop?*"

Like we said earlier, your habits should be customized and tailored to your goals; however, some habits have been proven to work for many successful people that you can also adopt:

- **Wake Up Early Every day**

Waking up early gives you an edge over other people who are late risers because it allows you some extra time that you can use to your own advantage. If you report to work by 9am daily and you wake up by 4am or 5am, it means that you have 4 or 5 hours before work and you can use those hours positively for exercise, meditation, and other things.

- **Create a To-do List Daily**

To-do lists are not an option for anyone who wants to be successful. To-do lists keep you accountable, and they keep you organized. Successful people are known to write their to-do lists a night before or every morning.

- **Meditate for 10 to 30 Minutes**

Meditation helps to rejuvenate your mind and body and puts you on the right track and taking care of your body and mind every day improves your chances of success.

- **Exercise Daily**

Exercise is not just for those who want to slim down or for people who want to build broad chests. Apart from helping you to stay fit and healthy, exercise improves the flow of blood to your brain, and that helps to improve your mental performance at work.

- **Delegate**

Successful people are picky about the tasks that they handle themselves. They handle the low effort, high reward tasks or the high effort, high reward tasks on their own, while they delegate the high effort, low reward or low effort, low reward tasks to others.

- **Eat a Healthy Breakfast**

Another thing that helps to increase your productivity is having a healthy breakfast daily. Your brain needs nutrients to perform optimally, and one of the ways to fuel up your brain for the day's job is to eat a healthy breakfast.

- **Sleep for 7 Hours**

After a hard day's job, you need to give your body some time to relax and rejuvenate. Sleep time is when your body repairs some of its damaged cells including the brain cells, so when you don't sleep well; you deprive your body the opportunity to properly rejuvenate. This is counterproductive because you'll either break down at some point, or your productivity levels will reduce so it's best to always give your body at least 7 hours to sleep after a hard day's job.

- **Network**

Successful people know the importance of human capital. You'll always need people to patronize your business, give you referrals, tell you what the latest industry trends are, and help your business in one way or another. No business can thrive without human capital, and that's why successful people are always actively expanding their network.

So, draw a networking timetable for yourself, so you can add one new valuable person to your network weekly or monthly.

- **Read Motivational Books**

You need to keep yourself on track, especially at your low moments or on days when you're distracted or feeling low.

Successful people always have a library of motivational books that they read from to help them learn more and stay focused.

- **Talk to Your Mentor**

Your mentor is someone who is very close to whom/what you want to be and you can gain a lot of valuable tips and ideas from them, or even understudy them and copy some of their own habits so make it a habit to keep in touch with your mentor as often as you can afford to.

- **Listen to Motivational Material**

You might not have the time to read, especially if you have a hectic schedule, but there's always time to listen to audios.

You can listen when driving or when you're doing your morning exercise, cooking, etc.

- **Prioritize Savings**

Savings and investments are tied together and there's no getting wealthy without both. Your savings are what you'll invest, and that means the more you save, the more you can invest, so it's essential to build a strong savings habit and put money away weekly, daily, or monthly towards achieving your goals.

- **Limit TV Time**

Successful people know that Television is an innovation that has the potential to waste your time and limit your productivity.

According to Thomas Carley, the author of *Rich Habits: The Daily Success Habits of Wealthy Individuals, "67% of rich people only watch TV for an hour or less per day"*.

Develop a strict TV habit and limit your TV time to the barest minimum.

- **Limit Social Media Time**

Social media is also a massive source of distraction. Social media is filled with people who are prepared to waste your time for the rest of the day, engaging you in meaningless chats and keeping you busy watching unproductive videos and photos.

Social media should be for leisure and limited to leisure times only, and that should not take more than one hour daily.

- **No When, and How to Say No**

Successful people are strict with their time, energy, and resources, and they know when to say no to people, and to things that do not fit into their plans, programs, or budgets.

You can write to-do lists daily for the next 10 years, or write a budget every month for the next 10 years but if you don't know how to say no whenever someone makes a request that you have not planned for, you won't make much progress.

- **Manage Your Money Daily**

At the end of every day, you should be able to know what your net worth is. This will keep you motivated and encourage you to work harder and help you correct yourself whenever you're doing anything that may jeopardize your wealth.

- **Visualize**

Sometimes, the best way to keep yourself motivated is to continually visualize your goals. Dedicate a few minutes to visualizing your goals daily so that you'll always be reminded of the reason why you have to continue to work hard.

- **Update Your Goals Every day**

Don't just write down your goals and ignore them. You should always update your milestones daily. What have you done today to contribute to the overall achievements of your goals? Make it a habit to keep track of your progress every day.

- **Build Your Emergency Funds**

Lack of emergency funds is why a lot of people run into debts because when the emergencies happen, and you don't have the funds to take care of them, you would be left with no other choice than to use your credit card or get a loan.

So, make it a habit to add some funds to your emergency account as often as possible so that you can always have funds to fall back on during emergencies. And if there are no emergencies, you can still take out some of the funds and invest it and worthwhile projects.

- **Invest Regularly**

You don't have to wait until you have a lot of money in your account or until you get a windfall to invest. You can make it a habit to invest small sums of money regularly or channel funds into your investment savings account as often as possible.

- **Pay off Your Credit Card Bills Every Month**

Credit card debts attract very high-interest rates. At the end of the day, the costs of allowing your credit card debts to accumulate become unreasonably high because the funds you use to service the debt can be put to productive use. So, make it a habit to always pay off your credit card debts at the end of every month.

- **Live One Standard Below Your Income**

Always live one standard below your current income so that you can always have enough money to save and invest. If you can afford to buy a 2-bedroom, buy a 1-bedroom and save or invest the rest of the funds.

- **Always Make and Follow Your Budget**

Budgeting is an excellent financial management tool, and it helps to prevent impulsive spending. It is essential to always use a budget to plan how to spend your income so that you can always use your financial resources judiciously and avoid waste.

- **Travel Often**

Traveling broadens your mind and perception. It inspires you and allows you the opportunity to expand your network. Traveling can also create business opportunities and help you relax, so make it a habit to travel to other locations as often as you can.

- **Learn a New Skill Often**

Until the day you die, you should never stop learning new skills. Learning new skills helps you grow and expand and become a better version of yourself. So as often as you can- whether daily, weekly or monthly, try to learn a new skill.

- **Manage Your Time Wisely**

Time management is essential. One of the contributing causes of failure or low productivity is poor time management. The more time you have to work, the more productive you'll become so always manage your time wisely, especially by using a to-do list.

- **Be Strict With Social Media**

Like we said earlier, social media is a serious time waster. According to recent research by Nielsen Group, *"American adults spend more than 11 hours per day watching, reading, listening to or simply interacting with media"*.

Imagine spending 11 hours a day on something that holds no financial or other benefits for you. If you're not earning income via social media, you should not be spending more than 1 hour daily on social media-make a strict schedule.

- **Look for Ways to Cut Back on Your Expenses Regularly**

You shouldn't do the *"I'm rich, so I don't need a bargain"* thing. Wealthy people don't get wealthy by throwing their money away; they get wealthy by actively growing their money so, at all times, you should consistently find alternatives, cut costs and reduce the prices you have to pay for goods and services.

- **Surround Yourself with People Who are What You Want to Be**

Always do an audit on the people around you and take note of the effect that they have on you. You've been friends with Mike for a month now, so how is Mike rubbing off on you? Are you learning good habits or bad ones from Mike? Sometimes, you can easily prevent yourself from forming bad habits when you regularly take stock of your friends and the people you hang out with.

- **Invest in Your Looks**

Looking good is not vanity- looks matter a lot. People have to get close to you before they discover your personality; what they see first is your looks, and it may be unfair, but most people judge you by your looks first before anything else.

This is why it is very important to always look good. Take time out every day to plan your outfit for the next day or the next week; don't just pick the first thing that stares at you in your wardrobe.

- **Make Sleep a Priority**

It is essential to sleep for at least 7-8 hours every day. Sleep time is when your body can cleanse itself, and repair damaged or spent cells, especially the brain cells, so giving yourself enough time to sleep helps your brain to stay sharp.

- **Don't Multitask While Eating**

Multitasking when eating makes you eat a little more than you should. It helps to do away from everything else and concentrate on eating during feeding times.

- **Use a Fitness App to Track Your Fitness**

There are mobile apps that help you track your fitness levels. It takes your daily feeding patterns and exercise routines into consideration, and tells you when you are gaining weight or losing weight, whether you are exercising enough and warns you when you are likely to gain weight from eating too much or not doing enough exercise.

Some of these apps include JEFIT (Android, iOS: Free), ClassPass (Android, iOS), and Workout Trainer (Android, iOS: Free). You can search for the top relevant apps for your favorite app store.

- **Have a Healthy Smoothie for Breakfast**

Smoothies are packed with fiber and healthy nutrients that can help to nourish your body and strengthen your body and brains for the day's job.

- **Plan Your Meals for The Week**

Planning your meals ahead helps to prevent unhealthy food choices.

- **Do Strength Training**

Strength training helps to build your muscles, and the more muscles you have, the faster your metabolism will be.

- **Have Daily Brainstorming Sessions**

Try to sit quietly in a place for a few minutes with your pen and paper in hand. A lot of ideas can come to you that way.

- **Practice Gratitude**

Every day, write down 2-3 things that you are grateful for. It really helps you appreciate your life and achievements and helps to keep you encouraged when things are not going well.

- **Laugh**

Watch, read, or listen to something that can make you laugh every day. Laughter is good for releasing tension and triggering the release of feel-good hormones.

- **Don't Drink Your Calories**

Avoid fizzy drinks, soda, or anything that doesn't fill you up but contains high amounts of calories.

- **Replace Carbs with Proteins at Every Meal**

Carbohydrates are not evil; they are essential for proper body growth and development but eating excessive amounts of carbs could be dangerous for the body. It can cause you to gain weight excessively, and increase your chances of suffering from insulin resistance or even diabetes.

Conclusion

We have come to the end of the book. Thank you for reading and congratulations on reading until the end.

There are no secret formulas for success in life. Even if you get lucky and win the lottery, you would still need good habits to manage the money you won. Everything boils down to your habits; your habits will make or break you.

As Aristotle aptly put it, "We are what we repeatedly do. Excellence, then, is not an act, but a habit." Or, put more simply: "Excellence is a habit."

If you found the book valuable, can you recommend it to others? One way to do that is to post a review on Amazon.

Please leave a review for this book on Amazon!

Thank you, and good luck! Ray & Ruby

www.ingramcontent.com/pod-product-compliance
Lightning Source LLC
Chambersburg PA
CBHW071735020426
42331CB00008B/2042